Frog Fight

A play by Julia Donaldson

Illustrated by Oliver Lake

Characters

Duck: Quack, quack! I'm hungry, Goose. Are you hungry too?

Goose: Yes, I'm **very** hungry.

Duck: Look! There's a little frog. It looks good to eat.

Frog: Oh no! Help!

Goose: I've got you, Frog. Now I'm going to eat you!

Duck: That's not fair. I saw the frog first.

Frog: Help! Let me go! You don't want to eat me – I taste disgusting!

Goose: Look, here comes Cat.

Cat: Miaow! What's all the fuss about?

Duck: Goose has got my frog. It's not fair!

Goose: It's not your frog. I caught it, so it's mine!

Cat: Well, now it's going to be **mine!** Got you, Frog!

Frog: Help, help! Put me down!

Duck: Look, here's Fox.

Fox: What's all the fuss about?

Goose: Cat's got my frog. It's not fair!

Duck: It's not your frog, it's **my** frog. I saw it first!

Cat: I've got it now, so it's mine.

Fox: You're all wrong. Got you, Frog!

Frog: Help! Put me down! I'm far too thin and bony to eat!

Cat: Give it back!

Goose: No, give it to me!

Duck: No – to me!

Fox: Why should I? I'm hungry.

Cat: Look, here comes Lion. He'll sort this out.

Lion: What's all the fuss about?

Cat: Fox has got my frog!

Duck: It's not yours, it's mine!

Goose: No, it's mine!

Fox: They're all wrong. It's mine!

Lion: Stop arguing and tell me what happened. Then I can be the judge.

Duck: Well, Sir, I saw this little frog.

Goose: And I caught it. But then Cat grabbed it.

Cat: And then Fox stole it from me.

Fox: So now the frog belongs to me.

Frog: No I don't! I don't belong to anyone! Put me down!

Lion: Put the frog down and let me think.

Goose: Oh no! You'll just let Duck have the frog because she saw it first.

Lion: I wasn't going to say that.

Duck: No, I bet you'll say that Fox should keep the frog.

Lion: I wasn't going to say that.

Cat: No, you'll say that **you'll** take the frog because we can't agree.

Lion: I wasn't going to say that.

Fox: No, you're too clever for that. You'll give the frog to Duck and Goose. Then you'll let Cat eat them. Then you'll let me eat Cat. And then you will eat me!

Lion: You're all wrong. Now let me speak, and hear what I **do** have to say.

Goose: So, what have you decided?

Lion: The little frog has hopped away. You'll just have to catch another one!